JOE
Wants To Be Famous

A story by Clara Lim

Illustration by Octaviani Isabella

For ages 2-5

tots PUBLISHING

content transcends technology

This is Joe. "Hello!" Joe says.

Joe is a double-decker bus that gives rides to the people of Sunnydale.

One day, the Bus Captain has exciting news for the fleet of buses. "The Mayor is coming to this bus depot!" he says.

"He wants to give the
cleanest bus a blue ribbon!"

Joe is excited!

He wants to win the blue ribbon so that everyone will look at him and he will be famous.

"I'll be the cleanest bus!" Joe calls and honks his horn.

The other buses are excited too, "No! I'll be the cleanest!" shouts Millie.

Joe decides he has to be very
careful on his route to be the
cleanest bus.

He cannot hit any railings
to avoid scratches.

He cannot drive through
mud so that it will not splatter
on his paint.

Joe drives very carefully
through the town.

"OH NO!" Joe cries.

He's just driven through a
dirty puddle! Yuck!

Joe now has a spot on
his shiny red paint.

Joe is sad, but has an idea.

If he can make the other buses
dirtier than him,
he can still win the ribbon!

Joe decides to speed through his route and dirty the other buses.

He sees Millie and splashes muddy water on her!

He sees Ben and drives
so close that Ben is
forced to hit a railing!

He sees Frank and honks so loudly that the painters on the nearby building splash paint on Frank in shock!

Joe goes back to the bus depot
very pleased with himself.

The other buses must be much
dirtier than him now.

He is sure to win the blue
ribbon and become famous.

The Mayor and Bus Captain stand in front of the fleet and are very disappointed.

"I see that you all are very dirty," says the Bus Captain.

"And Joe you are the dirtiest!"
says the Mayor.

Joe was so busy making the other buses dirty that he forgot to be careful.

He is even dirtier than the other buses!

"What happened, Joe?"
asks the Mayor.

"I'm sorry. I wanted to win the ribbon so I splashed mud on Millie...

...caused Ben to scratch his paint...

...and got paint all over Frank."

"I'm sorry, Millie. I'm sorry, Ben.
I'm sorry, Frank!"

"Well, Joe, we'll accept your apology if you promise never to do that again and help with cleaning the fleet."

Joe helped, and the Mayor gave him a pat on the back for being an honest bus.

The Mayor also gave the blue
ribbon to the fleet because they
were honest and hard workers.

The buses were so happy that they let out a great cheer!

"Hip-hip-HORRAY!"

tots PUBLISHING

content transcends technology

Other stories in this series:

CHARLIE gets stuck !

PERCY the angry fire engine

TOTS PUBLISHING

Every child deserves the best education.

Enhancing children's development, making learning fun! Tots Publishing helps to spark young ones to think, do and express themselves as they learn.

Fun educational applications

Phonics Train

Speed Flashcard

Letter Race

Animal Matching

See the full list of applications at
totsapps.com

ISBN 978-981-08-9415-3

90000 >

9 789810 894153

www.ingramcontent.com/pod-product-compliance
Lightning Source LLC
Chambersburg PA
CBHW042116040426
42449CB00002B/56